The Hummingbird Story

Lori Josifek

WestBow Press books may be ordered through booksellers or by contacting:

WestBow Press
A Division of Thomas Nelson & Zondervan
1663 Liberty Drive
Bloomington, IN 47403
www.westbowpress.com
844-714-3454

Interior Image Credit: self illustrated

KJV:
• Scripture taken from the King James Version of the Bible.

ISBN: 978-1-6642-1096-7 (sc)
ISBN: 978-1-6642-1095-0 (e)

Library of Congress Control Number: 2020921463

Print information available on the last page.

WestBow Press rev. date: 12/18/2020

WESTBOW
PRESS®
A DIVISION OF THOMAS NELSON
& ZONDERVAN

For my husband, Doug, who believes in me without reservation,

and for my four fledglings, Jenni, Isaac, Kacie, and Hannah

who successfully flew from my grasp when the time was right.

Dear little children, I have a true story to tell you. I tell it, so you will know that God loves you very, very much!

One day, as I was looking for my kitty, I spotted him way up high, on top of the trellis where the trumpet vines grow. "Here kitty, kitty, kitty ... come here Linus James!"

At once, Linus James made his way down the trellis to the patio below. As soon as I saw him, I knew that something was wrong! Protruding from the side of my kitty's mouth I saw tiny bird feathers.

Quickly, I picked up Linus James and held him close to me. Ever so carefully, I pried open his mouth. Into my hand fell the tiniest, most beautiful little hummingbird I had ever seen.

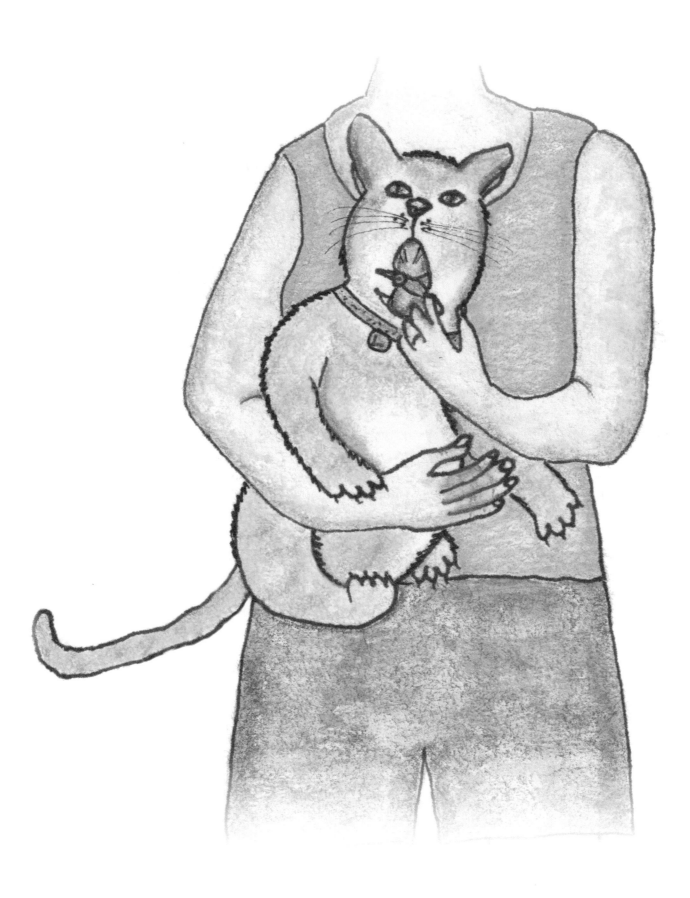

Its feathers were a shimmery blue, and from the tip of its wispy tail to the end of its pointy beak, the bird was barely two inches long. The delicate eyes were closed, and it lay so very still. Instinctively, I took the hummingbird into the house - away from Linus James.

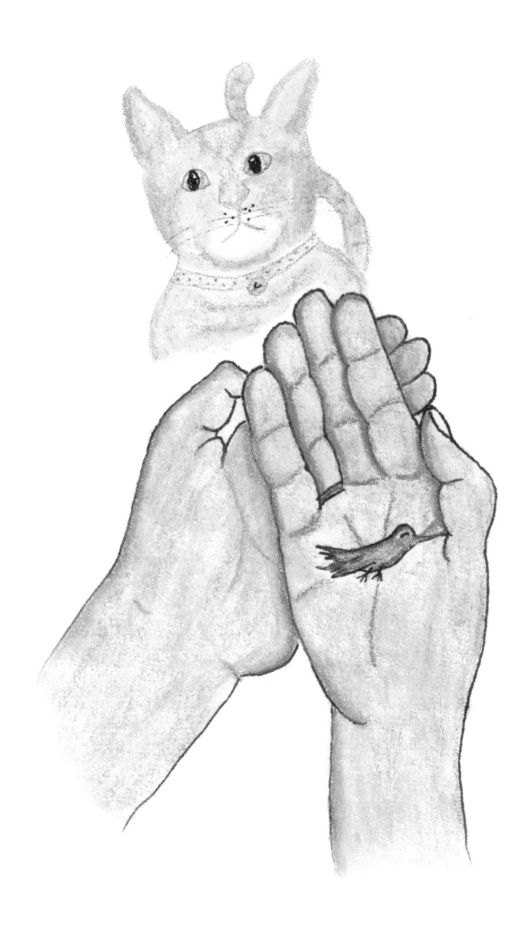

As I stared at this fragile creature, I thought I might have felt a faint movement. "Dear God," I prayed, "the Bible says that not one sparrow can fall to the ground without You knowing about it. This little baby hummingbird is much tinier than a sparrow, and You created it so beautifully. Please let it live," I pleaded.

Only a moment passed before I felt another slight tremble in my hand. Then, suddenly, the blue wings spread apart from its body and it began to flutter about. Quickly, I formed my hands into a protective cup around my little friend, and made my way to the front door.

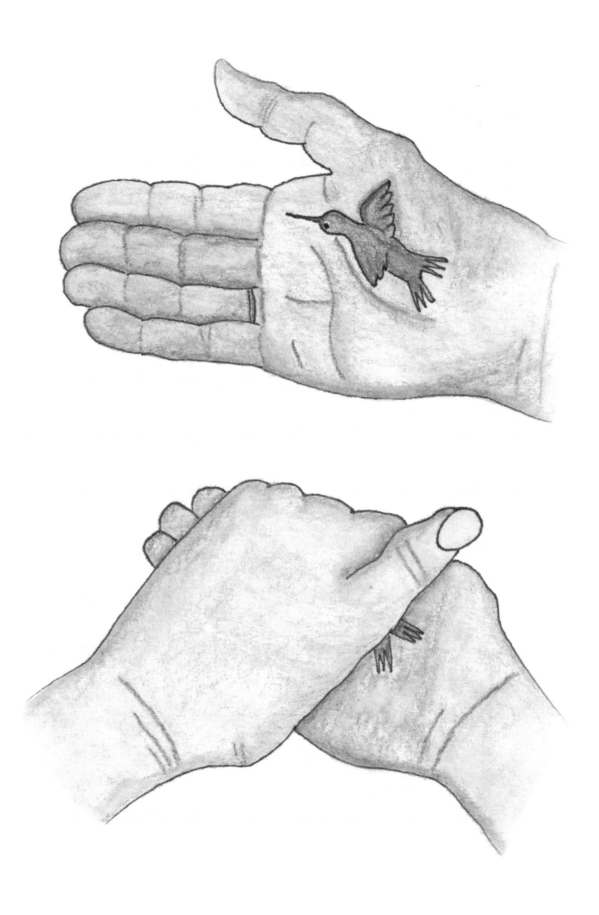

Once outside again, I opened up my hands, held them up high, and said, "Fly little bird!"

Without any hesitation, the bird flew up and away. A tear rolled down my cheek as I realized what a wonderful miracle had just happened. "Thank you dear God, for hearing my prayer and giving new life to that beautiful little hummingbird. If You care so much about such a tiny creature, how much more You must care about me!"

Little children, whenever you are sad, or sick, or lonely, or afraid ... remember what God has told us in His Holy Book, the Bible: "Are not two sparrows sold for a farthing? And one of them shall not fall on the ground without your Father. The very hairs of your head are numbered. Fear not, therefore; you are of more value than many sparrows." (Matthew 10:29-31)

whether it is a hummingbird, a sparrow, or you...God is watching an

Follow the hummingbird to a song you can learn and sing.

His Eye Is on the Sparrow

1. Why should I feel dis-cour-aged, ___ Why should the shad-ows come, ___
2. "Let not your heart be trou-bled," ___ His ten-der word I hear, ___
3. When-ev-er I am tempt-ed, ___ When-ev-er clouds a-rise, ___

why should my heart be lone-ly, ___ And long for heav'n and home, ___ When
And rest-ing on His good-ness, ___ I lose my doubts and fears; ___ Though
When songs give place to sigh-ing, ___ When hope with-in me dies, ___ I

Je-sus is ___ my por-tion? ___ My con-stant Friend ___ is He: ___
by the path ___ He lead-eth, ___ But one step I ___ may see: ___ } His
draw the clos-er to Him, ___ From care He sets ___ me free: ___ }

23

eye is on the spar-row, And I know He watch-es me; His

eye is on the spar-row, And I know He watch-es me. I

sing be-cause I'm hap-py, I sing be-cause I'm free, For His

eye is on the spar-row, And I Know He watch-es me.

Words by Civilla D. Martin, 1905
Tune by Charles H. Gabriel

24

About the Author

Lori Josifek has worn many hats in her life as a wife, mother, grandmother, teacher, choir director, artist, and writer. Devoting her life to teaching music, writing, and poetry, among many subjects, Lori has freely spread her wealth of arts to children outside the conventional education system for more than thirty-five years.

In her university years, Lori pursued a career in education and earned a teaching credential but did not stay in the public-school system long. After marriage and having four children, her goals refocused to providing home education to her children. Under her discipline, they earned a structured and full education beginning with music lessons around the piano every morning, Bible study and academic principles following, physical education in the afternoon, and "homework" to be completed before the next day.

During these years, Lori was inspired to start a children's choir whose presentations ministered at elderly facilities. When her children graduated on to higher education, Lori continued to teach writing classes to homeschooled children in the community.

Her writing is succinct, yet thoughtfully artistic as she paints a gentle message of her testimony of faith in her storytelling. Many of her stories and poems are inspired by her love of nature and the numerous pets who enriched her family life over the years. Lori lives in Chico, California, with her husband and enjoys tandem bicycling, rollerblading, camping, cooking, and spending time with her family.

Printed in the United States
by Baker & Taylor Publisher Services